A Crystal Spring Thanksgiving

A Little Girl Plays "Manly" Golf

T Michael White MD

ISBN: 1490333150
ISBN-13: 978-1490333151

Library of Congress Control Number: 2013910131
CreateSpace Independent Publishing Platform
North Charleston, South Carolina

Dedication

Just as sweet Maddie's story is published (born), a best friend has passed. At once, I am remembering our first meeting on the golf course and then years of planning and celebrating professional and personal successes walking about 18 holes. He would always say, "After 18 holes, the game tells you all you need to know about the man." It is so true. In our first round, I understood dapper attention to detail, diagnostic acumen, strategic brilliance, classy elegance, compassion, courage, dedication, devotion, generosity, honesty, integrity, kindness, a humble self-depreciating sense of humor and leadership in which to invest and forever follow.

Therefore, *A Crystal Spring Thanksgiving* is dedicated to the nexus of golf and life. Pursue the game. Grow in body, mind and spirit.

Dr. Mike White

Forewords

In *A Crystal Spring Thanksgiving,* the reader is treated to a heart-warming account of a proud grandfather quietly teaching his granddaughter important lessons about life and character through a "manly" golf match. To those who allow it, the game of golf can be a powerful instructor in life's lessons. When a masterful teacher is added to the mix, the lessons can be amplified and refined. In the story, we see Old Dad working his magic as family educator as he nudges young Maddie along her pathway to emotional maturity, just as he has done for the generation before her.

Familial love, spirituality, warm family tradition — all woven into a delightful short story — what's not to like? There is much to learn about golf, life, leadership and love in this story. I therefore enthusiastically commend it to your reading. Please enjoy reading *A Crystal Spring Thanksgiving* as much as I have.

Dr. Edward Drawbaugh
Physician Executive and Professional Photographer
Hagerstown, Maryland

On the surface, *A Crystal Spring Thanksgiving* is a captivating story about a young child and her grandfather experiencing a special day of golf. But as a devoted golfer (I do try my best) and business executive, I recognize it is so much more. In a heart-warming way, it portrays love, family, tradition, respect, professionalism and wisdom and the gentle teaching and learning of leadership and healthy competition. For me, the author parlays his career as mentor to so many patients, medical students and physicians in training, his devotion to his family and his comprehension of human psychology into a golf parable which may enable young people to excel in life. From my perspective as a mother, grandmother, great-grandmother, medical education professional and humble golfer, *A Crystal Spring Thanksgiving* is a message to be read and re-read by adults and explained to children and grandchildren so they may successfully make their way to the first tee and beyond.

Ms. Margie Kleppick
President and CEO, Partners in Medical Education, Inc.
Irwin Pennsylvania

Mike White is, at his core, a skilled teacher and a beloved mentor to many. In *A Crystal Spring Thanksgiving*, he deftly shares his gifts.

Golfers like Mike are romantics. How else could one explain a person's lifelong pursuit of the unachievable? We as golfers envision the glories of Jack Nicklaus while playing like Jack Lemmon.

A late season round of golf is the perfect setting for competition, tradition, wisdom and loving relationships. This story is penetratingly familiar because we know Maddie, Old Dad and the other characters. They are our families and they are in fact, us. *A Crystal Spring Thanksgiving* gloriously captures the, sometimes forgotten, moments we've lived and the lessons taught and learned which are always joyously revisited.

Dr. White has penned an elegant masterpiece, as rich in love as in life lessons. After all, life, like golf, is about timeless experiences and shared stories.

Charley Price
President, McConnell's Fine Ice Creams
Santa Barbara, California

As a PGA Professional and son of a PGA Professional, reading *A Crystal Spring Thanksgiving* reignited vivid memories of playing endless "manly" summer golf matches against my father and older brother. I grew up on

the golf course where I learned the life lessons that made me the man I am today. *A Crystal Spring Thanksgiving* is for all of those who never had the opportunity that our heroine, Maddie, or I have had. Now, as a father of two young children, I hope they find and embrace, through tales like this one and timeless moments on the course with family, friends and competitors, the lessons *A Crystal Spring Thanksgiving* illustrates. This book should be in every golfing parent and grandparent's library.
James Schouller Jr.
PGA Professional, Fountain Head Country Club
Hagerstown, Maryland

Fifty years ago, my father introduced me to the game of golf because, as he told me, "You may play by yourself or enjoy it in the company of others and pursue it for a lifetime." *A Crystal Spring Thanksgiving*, wonderfully written and beautifully illustrated, evokes fond memories of my favorite "firsts" on the golf course with my dad – the first time I outdrove him, the first time I beat him over 9 holes and the first time I beat him in an 18 hole match. I remember the pressure of those critical moments where the outcome of the match hung in the balance and the pride I felt when I finally stepped up to the next level. I can also vividly recall his bittersweet reaction — the pain of losing at anything AND the intense pride that came with his whispered exclamation, "That's my boy." Whether you are Maddie, Uncle Colin, Old Dad, my dad or a little bit of all four, this story is sure to please the golfer, competitor, caddie, mentor, coach, parent and child in all of you.
Dr. Brian Wong
Head Coach and CEO, The Bedside Trust
Seattle Washington

.

Introduction

As a writer, I am a good doctor. As a golfer, I am a good doctor. So how is it that this physician has set out to write a golf story? I do not fully understand the answer, but the following may begin to shed some light. As I have progressed through the tunnel of life (I am now a young 66 — the "new" 66 if you will), I am beginning to recognize:

- Life (spirit, person, family, profession) is an infinite exercise in learning and teaching and learning towards the perfection of the advancement of body, mind and spirit. This somewhat clumsy learning and teaching and learning label reflects in the process the teacher is learning — often learning the most.

- Golf at once brings our spiritual, physical, mental and mystical worlds together.

- Golf eliminates generation gap. In its timelessness, through shared experience and language, it provides old and young a common culture that enables the exploration (learning and teaching and learning) of values.

- Golf is egalitarian. Successful negotiation of the gentle but certain demands of course etiquette and fair play, from bag drop through the pub, by player or by caddie, directly translates to success with self, family, friends, co-workers, supervisors (yes, we all have supervision) and customers (some called patients). Comfort with the complex demands of the course, is only a small step from comfort with boardroom complexity and life.

- There is something inherent in the human genome that carries the past and its lessons learned and taught into our present. At times, I sense our genome somehow (a mystery to me) has lessons learned, taught and learned in the future on board too — a déjà vu thing? True immersion into golf — into focused competition and nature and away from the ceaseless barrage of the 21st century — enables this connectedness to manifest.

Do I have a goal for this undertaking? Upon reflection, I have several. I desire to write it (humbly done) and publish it (easily done in this day and age). I would be pleased if a senior golfer might read and enjoy it just for what it is. I would be elated if he/she found it worthy to share the sense of the story with a child or grandchild. And, I would be fulfilled if a young person were to be stimulated to become connected with golf and in the process found her/himself connected with the wisdom (learning, teaching, learning) of a parent, a grandparent, the past and/or the future.

At this time, I find myself on and challenged by a steep golf/life learning curve. Therefore, I will be pleased to hear from you regarding errors, omissions and opportunities for improvement. I look forward to growing from your insights. I will be better for it.

Respectfully submitted,
Mike
mikewhitemd@gmail.com

Prologue

My name is Dr. E (Elizabeth) Madeline Black Sullivan. Because I am a doctor, I have kept my maiden name (Black). As this Thanksgiving approaches, I am a 40 year old lady, but this week I am remembering perfectly being a 10 year old girl.

As an adult woman, I wear several hats. I am a wife to my husband John Sherman Sullivan — we call him Sherm. He is our handsome and talented writer, musician, artist, golf champion and stay-at-home dad. I am the mother of three. Our sweet daughter Emma is six. Our becoming adorable son, Arthur, is four and our jolly beagle, Abbey Beagle Sullivan, is three.

I am a physician and psychiatrist. I care for adults at the nearby university hospital. After attending the Naval Academy (like my dad), I went to medical school and then trained in psychiatry.

My grandfather, Dr. W Ryder Black, whom I called Old Dad, was also a physician. He is largely the reason I became a doctor. In his younger years, he was an adult medicine specialist and in his later professional years a medical educator and then a hospital medical director. When he retired from medicine, he wrote and published stories about medicine, golf and life as T Michael White MD "because Mark Twain was already taken." For almost 40 years, he and his elegant wife (my grandmother), Jacquelyn, lived along the famous Donald Ross-like Crystal Spring Golf Club's par 5, 17th hole. To this day, there is a controversy about who designed the course. Although it has the character of – and plays like – a Donald Ross course and he is known to have walked the land, the course's architect remains a mystery. Their home was a stately Richmond Colonial which their children named "The Crystal Spring WhiteHouse". It was a beautiful and magical place that opened warmly at the holidays for limitless family, friends and good times. There always seemed to be enough room and true adventure for everyone. Looking back, it is fair to say that their home provided the backdrop for many of my favorite childhood memories.

Grandmother Jackie died last spring at 87. Until her end, she had been spry and energetic. Then Old Dad, after what he judged "a great life," suddenly passed in the late summer. He was 92. Unexpectedly, they willed their magnificent home to me as "the lady/doctor/golfer/ mom who will best maintain and advance our family's Crystal Spring WhiteHouse traditions."

Old Dad had a special place in the home where he wrote his prose. It was a "manly" sitting room off the master bedroom that was brilliant with light from two skylights and a bay window that owned "his" golf course. He called this room his writer's garret. It housed his lovingly scratched Scandinavian desk, his battered leather love seat, his treasured books and his orderly files. Prominently displayed was a framed Joe Kaye picture of his favorite place away from his Crystal Spring WhiteHouse — Shelving Rock at the entrance to the Lake George narrows as seen from the ancient Sagamore Hotel's promenade.

As a prerequisite for taking ownership of the house, his will required me to "dedicate one week to the review and organization of W Ryder Black/T Michael White's papers and manuscripts" and to "submit logical documents to Dr. Black's beloved alma mater — Schenectady's Union University." So last week, in preparation for moving in this week — curiously the week before Thanksgiving — I organized Old Dad's files. As I began to sift through his papers, a story with a hand-written note was prominently on top. Old dad's surprisingly legible printed note read:

A Crystal Spring Thanksgiving

Crystal Spring WhiteHouse
July 2012

My dearest Maddie,

Someday, when I move on, please help me connect our family's wonderful past with our family's promising future. Care has been taken to ensure that what follows is true to what you told me the Friday after our still famous "manly" Crystal Spring Golf Club Thanksgiving Day match. Please ask your wonderful mate and our resident artist, Sherm, to create a few illustrations (hawk, beagle, Indian, settler, coin, #10 flag, scorecard, etc.). Then insist Union University, as a prerequisite for the gift of my papers (which they may be interested in) and my significant contribution to its endowment fund (which they will be interested in), publish the work as a short story for child and grandparent golfers. More importantly, each year when you compete in the lady's club championship and then when your Emma competes in the lady's club championship, feel my presence as I (and your colonial settlers and Native Americans) will be there with you.
Love,
Doctor/Writer/Golfer/Mister/Dad/Old Dad/Sir

Suddenly, it was 1982 and I was ten again. My family and I were living in Hawaii where my dad, Lieutenant Commander B (Benjamin) Ryder Black was the Navy pilot for the Chief of Naval Operations in the Pacific. As a special treat, I was the only grandchild invited to the Crystal Spring WhiteHouse for this Thanksgiving. Old Dad was still the medical director at the hospital. My Aunt Cait (Catherine),

Uncle Brian (her husband) and my Uncle Colin were coming in from Washington, DC for the holidays. Old Dad and I were to compete formally in an official "manly" 9-hole Crystal Spring Golf Club Thanksgiving Day golf match.

E Madeline Black MD
November 2012

A Crystal Spring Thanksgiving

A Little Girl Plays "Manly" Golf

Ability — that which you are capable of doing.
Motivation — that which determines what you do.
Attitude — that which determines how well you do it.
Coach Lou Holtz

Thanksgiving 1982

Good Thanksgiving Day morning from me — E (Elizabeth) Madeline Black. I am 10 years old. My grandfather says I am four foot something and pound for pound the best lady golfer in these 50 United States and Puerto Rico. I humbly identify with his sentiments. My grandfather says it is important to be humble.

I have traveled from Hawaii where I live with my family to celebrate Thanksgiving in Hagerstown, Maryland (I call it H-Town) with my grandparents. My brothers and sisters and I call them Old Dad and Jackie. *Note: never call Jackie Old Jackie as nothing good ever comes of that.*

My Aunt Cait and my Uncles Brian and Colin and I will enjoy Jackie's turkey and stuffing, twice mashed potatoes, sweet potatoes, cranberry sauce, pumpkin, apple and cherry pies and late night turkey and stuffing sandwiches on fresh white bread with too much mayonnaise and way too much salt. However, my primary reason for coming from Hawaii is to compete in a formal "manly" golf match against Old Dad on Thanksgiving Day. The match will be contested at the Crystal Spring Golf Club which is a famously proud and challenging course designed in 1920 — the same year my Old Dad was born.

Everyone calls me Maddie except Old Dad who calls me Elizabeth Madeline Black. He is a doctor, an author, a golfer and my grandfather. My dad (his son) is a Navy Aviator and golf champion who brought me up to call everyone one, including Old Dad, "Sir." Old Dad has further instructed me to call him "Doctor/Writer/Golfer/Mister/Dad/Old Dad/Sir"; but, I mostly call him Old Dad and mostly get away with it. Almost everyone else just calls him Doc.

If I have a good day on the course today, I will shoot 80 from the ladies' tees. If Old Dad has a great day he will shoot 85 from the men's tees. Therefore, it is reasonable to conclude that, on paper at least, Old Dad doesn't have much of a chance. With a bit of glee I feel sad, but not too sad, for Doctor/Writer/Golfer/Mister/Dad/Old Dad/Sir.

Sadie Beagle

Last night I put my gear in order. Sadie Beagle, Old Dad and Jackie's beautiful and loving black, white and a touch of brown beagle, was my helper and constant companion. She just loves to work. She was with me every step up and down the stairs as I cleaned my clubs, polished and marked my balls, gave my shoes a shine and made sure my golf glove, tees, ball markers and ball mark repair device were all in order.

By rule, I am allowed 14 clubs. I carry 5, 6, 7, 8, 9-irons; pitching, gap, sand and lob wedges; 3, 5, 7 woods, driver and my super special low-tech high-performance putter which I have named "Old One Putt." Old Dad carries the same except he replaces the lob wedge with a nine-wood. According to Old Dad, my dad, "Was playing 18 holes the day before he started to walk" and learned to count by counting Old Dad's irons: one-iron, two-iron up to nine-iron followed by pitching wedge, sand wedge. It took my dad another year to learn that 10 — and not pitching wedge — came after nine.

Whenever I am around, Sadie Beagle becomes my dog or as Jackie says, she adopts me as her human. She slept with me last night. This morning her gentle cold moist nose on my cheek woke me just in time

(as if she understood the rhythm and pace of this special day) to enjoy a perfect Jackie golf day "breakfast of champions" — a bacon, egg and cheese sandwich and oat meal with blueberries and banana — and complete my stretching exercises before heading for the course.

Jackie pressed and laid out my clothes for the big match. As she placed my hair in a golfer's braid, she said, "Win or lose you must look your best. Remember what Aunt Cait says, 'Looking good on the first tee starts you out under par.'"

At breakfast Old Dad gave me a big hug and wished me well today. He said I looked "fabulously beautiful" and "as cool as the other side of the pillow." Smiling, he added, "It's a shame that today you will experience a Thanksgiving thumping at the hands of an old master." To my surprise, joy and relief, my Uncle Colin, a young accountant and champion golfer, had come in from Washington DC for breakfast. With a smile, he whispered so Old Dad could not hear, "I will be your caddie and it is a shame that today we shall administer a Thanksgiving thumping to Doctor/Writer/Golfer/Mister/Dad/Old Dad/Sir."

Let me tell the story of the match just as I remember it happening.

Mental Gifts

When Uncle Colin and I arrive, the practice range is eerily quiet on this brisk, late autumn, holiday morning. We are alone. Old Dad has already stopped down, hit a few warm-up shots and moved on. I have now completed my standard 30 minute pre-match warm-up. Starting with the wedge, I have hit each of my clubs. My swing and all my shots are in order. Uncle Colin has me visualize the play of each of the nine tournament holes and I am birdieing each. He reminds me that as Old Dad had taught us "today is not about golf — it is about life." Today and every day, I must humbly be true to myself, tell myself the truth, be as good as my word, not be affected of others, not assign motives to the

behaviors of others and do my best. If I am humbly successful in this regard, my inner greatness will express itself.

My dad is a champion golfer. Old Dad entrusted my dad's swing to a young Mr. Joe Longo who went on to become a famous swing coach. My dad, with an occasional tweak from Major Jim, is responsible for my swing. However, my dad's and therefore my success on the course emanates from a series of Old Dad (he of the quirky swing) mental gifts to us:

- From my dad's earliest days, Old Dad made sure that the golf course was my father's favorite place. Family pictures show my dad, before he had learned to walk, joyfully crawling after Old Dad's and Jackie's putts on the practice green. Family pictures show a joyful me crawling after golf balls in my favorite place. From the very beginning Old Dad taught my dad that his strongest muscle was between his ears — his brain. My dad has convinced me my brain is my strongest muscle.

- Old Dad taught my dad that life, love, goal, work and golf are important four letter words that explain what our existence is all about and ensure that we are equal to every challenge. As the famous football coach Lou Holtz taught Old Dad, as Old Dad taught my dad and as my dad conveyed to me — my ability is what I am capable of doing, my motivation determines what I will do and my attitude determines how well I will do it.

Phenom

With great confidence, I head for the practice green which is adjacent to the first tee. As I approach the green, I am surprised to find quite a commotion. Jackie is here with an excited leashed Sadie Beagle. Aunt Cait and Uncle Brian, both young business executives in Washington DC and champion golfers have arrived. Some of Old Dad and Jackie's friends and some members of the club have turned out for the match. Several have brought their children and grandchildren along for the show. Suddenly reality sinks in — this is to be a major, formal "manly" golf event. My heart pounds and I have trouble getting my breath. Uncle Colin gently squeezes my shoulder and reminds me — "Be true to yourself." In his grip, I find my composure and move on to take a few practice putts remembering that putts that are short rarely go in. In the buzz, I hear people saying things like: "Hawaii," "10 years old," "phenom," "can such a tiny thing beat a grown man," and "this should be fun." I put it all out of my head and begin to concentrate on my game.

Uncle Colin looks me in the eyes and says, "Of one thing we can be certain — Old Dad will give it his best. If you beat him today, it will be fair and square. We can have every confidence that in a golf match, he will not give the Pope, Mother Theresa, Bambi, his sainted Grandmother Emma LaFountain Collins or a cute little distaff dynamo from Hawaii a six inch putt. This match will be all business today." Then he goes on to say, "He thinks that he and his caddie will be able to out think us two shots the front side. We cannot let that happen. Like them, we must be vigilant and thoughtful and apply our strongest muscle to each and every shot."

Silver Coin

At the appointed starting time, Uncle Colin and I approach the first tee. Mr. Major James 'Bolt' Landing II, the young club professional at Crystal Spring Golf Club is there with a microphone in his hands. The children may call him Major Jim or Mr. Landing but never 'Bolt.' The adult members call him 'Bolt' — a nickname that caught on when he was in college because of his lightning-like stingers off the tee. He is Old Dad's teacher, he is always sweet to me and, at Old Dad's insistence, he keeps a close eye on my swing and my game. With a hearty smile and handshake, he warmly welcomes Uncle Colin and me and makes us feel truly at ease.

My opponent, Old Dad, is already on the tee. He looks calm, fit and young for his 62 years. He is perfectly dressed — Aunt Cait's influence no doubt — and quite handsome with matching cap, golf shirt, wool sweater and corduroy slacks. And then I see his caddie — my dad.

Anticipating my surprise, he has a big grin on his face. Having come right from the airport, he has his aircraft carrier ball cap and his flight suit on. Old Dad says with a smirky smile, "The Navy has sent your Dad in on a special mission to caddie for me." "Maddie", says my dad as he picks me up and gives me a bear hug, "You are a great champion. Humbly walk the course with God today as will Old Dad and I. Play well. I love you very much and, win or lose, I will be very proud of you." And then Uncle Colin quietly says to me, "Old Dad is clearly worried as he has gone to great care and expense to bring your Dad, a master Navy strategic thinker, in for this match."

Just before we tee off, Old Dad comes over and places a silver ball marker/coin which has been especially minted for this Thanksgiving Day match into my hand. On one side there is a likeness of me standing with my bag and clubs and Sadie Beagle at my side and it reads, "Elizabeth Madeline Black HSTBAGC 1982." On the reverse side of the coin is a figure of a young female golfer with a golfer's braid in the midst of a perfect swing — which looks a lot like mine — with the letters TDCT — TYS and HWTCWG. Later I would learn that Old Dad gave a similar silver coin to each family golf champion on the day of an important match. The messages were the same for each: on the front – humbly strive to be a great champion; and, on the back: trouble, distance, club, target – trust your swing and humbly walk the course with God.

Mistake

Major Jim makes an announcement over the loud speaker. "May I please have your attention?" Today's 9-hole Thanksgiving event will be match play. Strict USGA rules shall apply. In the event of a tie, the players will proceed to a sudden death tie breaker on the back nine starting with hole number 10 until a winner is determined. Teeing off first from the men's tees is Crystal Spring Golf Club's own 'almost' Senior Champion — 'If he could just once play his usual game' — Doc Black." The large assembled gallery lets out a friendly and affectionate roar for Old Dad

who confidently tees up his ball and strikes it mightily with his driver. It flies down the middle of the fairway and our match is underway.

Uncle Colin and I move to the forward ladies' tee with the gallery led by Sadie Beagle in close pursuit. Major Jim announces, "From Honolulu, Hawaii, Ms. Elizabeth Madeline (Maddie) Black" and the gallery is again warm and encouraging. With driver in hand, I tee up my ball, identify trouble, chose my target and trust my swing. The ball flies long and straight and Uncle Colin says, "Let the big dog hunt." I say to him, "We are off" and with the gallery excitedly following, we briskly walk forward to my next shot.

Old Dad is 150 yards away from an elevated green with the pin in the back left rear of a classic, tiny, wavy, deep-rough surrounded Donald Ross-like green. He hits an iron to the middle of the green. Uncle Colin instructs me to do the same, "Short or in the middle is the safe play." I do not listen and hit it as I would in Hawaii — right at the pin. My seven-iron is perfectly hit, lands right by the hole and bounds off the hard green into very deep, lush rough that encircles the rear of the green. Old Dad is away, just misses a long birdie putt and taps in for par. I struggle to chip from the Velcro-like rough, land the ball by the hole and then watch it roll way past to the front of the green. I miraculously sink a forty-footer for par and a tie. Uncle Colin sternly says, "You got away with a mistake there Sweet Pea. Old Dad is already snickering — it is right out of Chapter One of his scholarly tome, *Dumb Golf*. Learn your lesson and listen to me or Sadie Beagle will soon be carrying your bag." I understand his message—we are a team and together we have to out think Old Dad today. I realize that I am very fortunate to be even par after one hole and I become a very attentive, humble listener from this point forward.

We both drive down the middle of the fairway towards the 2nd hole. I am away and understand my target to be the right middle green and my trouble to be the Mr. Ross-like, scary rough in the back of another postage stamp green. I trust my swing and hit a five-iron as planned and have 15 feet for birdie. Old Dad puts a seven- iron in the same position.

Eyes Closed

Old Dad has taught all in the family (me too) to putt with eyes closed. After I study and determine the roll of my putt, I stand over the ball, close my eyes and envision the ball, rolling into the hole. As I strike the ball, I am free of distractions such allergic tears or the movement of leaves, bugs or people. My mind addresses only line, pace and getting it "cozy" (close). My mind provides me with a vision of the ball on course and rolling, rolling into the hole — a most powerful use of my most powerful muscle.

Although it is late November in H-Town, as we approach the par 5 3rd hole, it is a glorious day. Mid-morning, the sky is blue with several high, large, white clouds. The temperature is 55 (versus the Hawaii 82 to which I am accustomed). The wind is calm. My hands are warm. It is a perfect golf sweater day so my toasty, but cumbersome, mittens and jacket stay, at the ready, in my golf bag.

After an energetic, whispered conversation with his caddie, Old Dad successfully "goes for it" and drives over the trees and into the middle of the fairway which cuts the par 5 in half. He is likely to make the green in two. I have to play the dogleg as it was designed — driver, fairway wood and pitching wedge to the green. After following that formula, I am 15 feet away in three. Old Dad's second shot is a smooth five-wood that catches the bunker to the left of the green. He blasts out and then two putts for five. I two putt for five and the match remains all square.

The par 3, 4th hole holds little adventure. Old Dad hits a high fading seven-wood to ten feet and I hit five-wood to eight feet. We both make our putts for workmanlike birdies and head for the 5th tee. The gallery on the other hand is well aware the match is even and we are both two shots under par. Their enthusiasm begins to heat up and I become aware of a bit of a buzz. Somehow word has gone out to friends and neighbors and an already substantial gallery is beginning to increase in size.

I Feel Good

On the short par 5, 5th tee Old Dad says, "I am glad to see you came from Hawaii ready to play today" and then crushes a drive down the

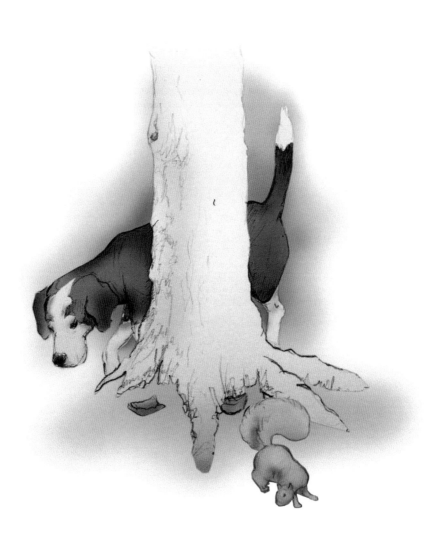

middle. As Uncle Colin hands me a driver, he says, "Don't fall for that Old Dad good sport mumbo jumbo." I answer, "I won't." Then, totally distracted by Old Dad's compliment, I hook my drive into the deep, luxuriant rough beneath the trees on the left.

The gallery is on the right side of the fairway and no one is quite sure where my ball landed. We search the deep grass for several minutes. Uncle Colin and I start to panic as we fear the consequences of not finding my ball — a penalty stroke, return to the tee and a certain loss of the hole to Old Dad. Then, on the other side of the fairway, Jackie frees Sadie Beagle from her leash and Sadie rushes across the fairway as if after a rabbit. After only a few seconds of beagle sniffing, snorting and tail-wagging yelping, her hunt is over. She stays in one spot, barks her alert and there, to everyone's surprise and delight, is my invisible number eight Callaway at the bottom of four inches of frosty, soggy rough which reminds Uncle Colin of "our neighbor's ungroomed soaking wet standard poodle." I wedge it out safely onto the fairway, hit a strong three-wood near the green, chip on and one putt for par. After a monster three-wood to the green, Old Dad is on in two, two putts for a birdie and the lead. I am now one down after five holes with only four left to play.

How do I stay calm when a shot and the match are moving in the wrong direction? In times of stress, my dad (taught by Old Dad) has taught me to sing James Brown's *"I Feel Good"* on my way to my next shot. No matter how dire my circumstance, the rhythm (especially the sax and rim shot interlude), energy and message of the song changes me, enables me to put the past behind and optimistically concentrate solely on my next shot — the Old Dad "play the game one shot at a time" thing. As I walk from my loss of the 5th hole towards the 6th tee, James Brown is with me. Upon arrival at the tee, "I feel nice." "I feel good."

Hector

At this time a huge hawk magnificently swoops low like a Navy jet from the oak tree behind the par 3 6th green and takes a perch in full

view high in a pine tree above our sixth tee. Old Dad says, "Hello Hector, welcome to the show. Perhaps you have an inkling that fireworks are about to ignite." Uncle Colin speaks quietly to me and says, "When Old Dad dies, he hopes to come back as a Crystal Spring hawk." I go right over to Old Dad and sassily say, "Someday I hope to fly like a hawk." With alarm, Uncle Colin says, "Why did you do that?" "To distract him," I proudly reply. Uncle Colin displays a worried frown and says, "He doesn't distract. He just turns from fierce to scary fierce."

The 6th hole is a very long and challenging par 3. The weather remains pleasant but a breeze is kicking up into our face making the hole play a club longer. Old Dad takes serious hold of a three-wood and sends it towards the pin. The ball is flying high, straight and true and seemingly forever. Uncle Colin gasps, "Look out. It is right on the money." The ball bounces once, hits the pin just above the hole and caroms wildly back 30 feet to the fringe at the front the green. Uncle Colin sighs, "We just dodged an Old Dad hole-in-one bullet and he got the worst break imaginable. He will struggle to get par from there." Across the tee, my dad gives Old Dad a supportive hug. The gallery is alive with excitement.

As I tee up my ball, splendidly powerful and huge Hector gracefully swoops from the pine tree and glides just above the fairway, over the green and without a flap of his wings, up to the top of the massive leafless oak tree behind the green. Again, he is perched high and in magnificent full view. My dad says, "The Navy could learn something about flying from that bird." Someone in the gallery says, "This is eerie. It is like that hawk is watching and enjoying this match." I settle in and hit my driver into the wind and directly at the pin. Uncle Colin yells, "Be the club" and my ball bounces once, rolls and rolls toward the cup and stops a half a revolution short of a hole-in-one. It seems as if the breeze is keeping the ball from falling in the hole. The gallery is at first stunned and then delirious over the two extraordinary shots they had just witnessed. Aunt Cait yells, "Now that's what I'm talking about." I run full speed to the green, take the pin out and tap the ball the final fraction of an inch into the hole for a birdie. Old Dad chips to within 8 inches and, after an acquiescing nod from Uncle Colin, I pick up his ball and concede his putt. I look up for Hector but he has flown off. I have evened the match. Old Dad and I are all square after six. Boy, do "I feel good."

Mission

Per Old Dad tradition, from time to time we young ones (children and then grand children) would be summoned to sit on his lap in a swivel chair in his East facing living room as the sun came up. From my earliest memories, I remember sitting "in conference" on Old Dad's lap in his warm early morning sunlit living room and his sharing his mentors' wisdom and its "application to life and golf." Over the years my brain expanded and his consistent messages increasingly sunk in. As we move "even" towards the 7th hole, I am instinctively aware:

- From his quality guru (Dr. Phil Crosby):
  - Golf is a process that can be studied and improved,
  - My definition of quality golf is my conformance to the etiquette, physical and technical requirements of the game,
  - My standard today (my mission; my attitude) is error free golf,
  - My system for quality golf is prevention — the continuous design and practice of the right way and
  - My measurement of the quality of my game is the cost of my mistakes — the manifestation of poor decisions and poor execution on my scorecard.
- From his education guru (Dr. David Leach), the golfer must master seven competencies:
  - Knowledge,
  - Execution,
  - Interpersonal Communications,
  - Professionalism,
  - Self-scrutiny and continuous improvement,

- o Teamwork and
- o Preservation of vitality through finding a balance between golf and life.
- From his spiritual/mystical guru (Dr. Brian Wong) the golfer must:
  - o Always tell him/herself the truth,
  - o Never assign motive to the behaviors of others,
  - o Never be influenced by the opinion of others,
  - o Always do her/his best and
  - o Remain eternally capable of change.

At this point, I am on a mission and playing quality golf. To the best of my ability to comprehend and comply, Old Dad's wisdom of the ages is with me. On the first, I escaped poor judgment and I know what Old Dad was thinking, "Poor judgment comes from a lack of experience and experience comes from poor judgment." On the 5th hole, a lack of concentration put me a hole behind. Then a miraculous shot on the 6th — am I lucky or good? (Byron Nelson's "The more I practice the luckier I get") — brought me even. Old Dad's sardonic, "This game is easy" rings in my ears. With rhythm and energy, "I feel good."

Crystal Spring

The 7th hole is a very long par 4 for the men and a short par 5 for the ladies giving me a most welcomed significant advantage here. One hundred yards before the green, a stream crosses the course, so I have to be sure to calculate my second shot to avoid getting wet. The stream starts as a spring from the cellar of a stone farmhouse built in 1750 which is just right of the fairway. Legend has it that the spring was historically named Crystal Spring and that the Western Maryland colonial settlers and local Native Americans took refuge in the farm house from the fierce invading French and Indians. As the story goes, the golf course takes its name from the crystal clear spring from which flows the coldest, purest water. From the farmhouse, the stream meanders into

Antietam Creek and then down to the site of the famous H-Town Civil War Battle on its way to the Potomac River, the Chesapeake Bay and the Atlantic Ocean.

Old Dad hits a long drive towards the farm house but stays safely in bounds just short of the creek. Uncle Colin hands me my driver and says, "Great champion, feel the strength and courage of the brave Native Americans and colonial settlers." With a sense of their presence, I coast to an easy par 5 and Old Dad struggles for a tough par 4 and we remain even after seven holes.

The breeze is picking up and the temperature is dropping. Uncle Colin observes, "Winter is in the air. I feel a storm brewing."

The eighth hole is a severe 90 degree dogleg right par 4. With my dad's encouragement, Old Dad again goes over the trees and has a nine-iron left to the green. I go straight out and have a long five-wood in. The story on this hole is the second shot. The green has a tiny flat area in the back and slopes down severely towards the front. The pin today is at the bottom in the front. The idea is to be short after two and to be putting uphill. Anything beyond the hole will mean a downhill putt that if missed will roll off the front of the green. Per Uncle Colin, "It will be like putting down a tilted ice skating rink." I hit my five-wood right at the pin and it rolls up and beyond. Just before it gets up to the hopeless back plateau (a dastardly position), it stops, changes direction and begins to roll back down towards the hole. As it picks up speed, it heads directly towards the flag, hits the pin, bounces off and goes down to the front fringe. Uncle Colin says, "We just missed a Maddie eagle from the fairway by a smidge. I officially do not believe what I am seeing." Old Dad and my dad are chuckling with incredulity. "Dodged an Elizabeth Madeline Black bullet there did I," says Old Dad. His nine-iron shot settles safely very near mine and we both make cozy first putts then tap in for our pars. As on any day, we are both pleased to escape the eighth with pars. As we head for the ninth tee, we remain all square.

Tips of the Caps

Major Jim is on the tee with a bull horn. His wife Riley and their young son, Trip (Master Major James Landing III, age 5), are at his side. From the 1ˢᵗ tee, they have been in the gallery and have followed our every step. Trip, with a fairway wood cut down to his size in hand — "just in case" — is particularly excited. He, of course, is rooting for me.

Suddenly, Major Jim becomes all business and announces, "Ladies and gentlemen, we are in the midst of a Crystal Spring Golf Club Thanksgiving Day match that would make the legends of golf proud. As the official scorer, I have each player at three under par and the match all square going into the final hole. The gallery and I wish to thank both players for this exciting exhibition today and we wish you the best as you two fine champions conclude this match." The gallery, which has now doubled in size, roars its approval. As I am taking it all in, Uncle Colin says, "Don't let your attitude impact your game and don't let your game impact your attitude." I understand his meaning, find truth in myself and walk calmly to the ninth tee.

In proportion to its importance, play at the ninth hole is steady but unexciting — two respectable drives, two worthy shots to the green and two sound two-putt pars. After our irons from the fairway to the middle of green, Uncle Colin hands me my putter and says, "It is time for Old Dad and you to enjoy well-deserved long walks with short sticks." Our two caddies quickly blend into the gallery. For a moment Old Dad and I are alone in the middle of the course. Then little Trip, with Sadie Beagle on her leash, joins us and leads us towards the ninth green and clubhouse. A huge, noisy crowd surrounds the green and another equally large and animated gallery peers down from the clubhouse deck. Although the wind is now up and the temperature has dropped significantly, their reception fills me with a warm glow. Old Dad says, "Tips of the caps are in order" — the first of my career — and he and I oblige. After our routine pars, there is sudden death golf to play.

Bunker

Major Jim says we are entitled to a 10 minute break before we head for the difficult par 4, 10th. With Aunt Cait standing guard at the entrance, Uncle Colin and I find some warmth in the ladies' locker room. I put on a turtleneck beneath my wool sweater and don my wool ski cap. No gloves for now (hands in my pockets between shots) as they only will complicate play.

Uncle Colin has me lay down on a bench and asks, "What is your favorite summer place?" I say, "Sunbathing on a pontoon boat anchored in Lake George's Paradise Bay." He says, "Go there," and for a few moments with my eyes closed, it is a hot summer day and as I am baking in the sun I am feeling the gentle bobbing of the boat on the lake. Then he says, "With your eyes closed, see driver down the middle, iron at the pin and one-putt for birdie and the win." On the fringe of a dream, I visualize each successful shot. Then I am awake and James Brown and I are rhythmically heading for the 10th tee and sudden death.

On the tee, Major Jim announces the playoff and there are big, warm hugs and high fives all around —Old Dad, my dad, Uncle Colin and me. Old Dad sends one long and straight down the middle. My red tee is far forward and after my sweet drive Old Dad is away. He hits his favorite club, "situation seven-wood" his "favorite number", to the middle of the green and it rolls towards the hole and stops 20 uphill feet from birdie. Since this is sudden death, Uncle Colin and I know I have to get it close. I hit a solid five-iron at the pin and it rolls just two inches too far, slopes off the back of the Mr. Ross-like green and drops into the back bunker 10 feet below the green. My always cool and always encouraging Uncle Colin mutters, "Death." Holding back tears, I plod towards the back bunker.

Here is the deal — I am in the bunker a good 10 feet below the green. The pin is just 10 feet from the edge of the green which slopes down and away from the bunker. Old Dad surely has his par 4 in hand (maybe birdie three) and, just to get out of this very deep bunker, I must

blast far beyond the hole and at best be left with a very long putt back uphill for par. Ugh! Uncle Colin is right — death by bunker.

Major Jim judges Old Dad is away. He putts for birdie. It just lips out and he taps in for his par. I go down into the bunker with Uncle Colin nearby. A constant wind is severely rocking the pin and the flag far overhead. The flag and its large number 10 are streaming perpendicular to the right above me. I turn back to Uncle Colin at the rear edge of the bunker. The gallery has assembled 20 yards behind him to watch my improbable shot.

Suddenly, I perceive a farrago of Native Americans and colonial settlers standing with Uncle Colin. A stately, very Scottish mustachioed gentleman in an immaculate wool suit, tie and plus fours, addressed by the ancients as "Mr. Ross", stands encouragingly there too. Trip and Sadie Beagle have moved up and stand with them. They are all amiably rooting me on. Without mentioning the implausible gallery company standing about him, I tell Uncle Colin what I am thinking — I am going to try and hit the wind-blown flag with hope the ball will drop down for a makeable putt and a tie to extend the match. Uncle Colin says, "I am not sure it has ever been done, but if it can be done, you are the "manly" golfer to do it." Despite his best effort, he sounds unconvincing.

Here is the rest of the deal — I have the ability to hit this shot from the bunker. My conscious brain is smart and knows what I should do — my motivation. And, my subconscious brain is most powerful and if my attitude is right, it will assist me with the implausible. How a ten year old girl knows this and why my champion golfer caddie has forgotten is a mystery. Now, in the midst of sand and wind, the courageous colonial settlers and Native Americans, along with a little boy and a beagle stand about me. They are optimistically smiling and giving me thumbs' up encouragement to go for it. Mr. Ross nods his agreement. I feel good.

I step up to the ball, dig my spikes into the sand, open my clubface, picture the flight of the ball and give it a go with as mighty a blast as I

have in me. The ball and the sand rise upward into the wind and, just as envisioned, the ball hits the wind-blown flag square in the middle. The flag tenderly caresses the ball – like a young child holding a baby robin fallen from his nest – ever so patiently holds it for a moment and then drops it gently to the left of the flag where spin and the brewing blizzard wind send it rolling, rolling towards and then into the cup for a sandy birdie three — and a sudden-death win.

My brave Native Americans, courageous colonial settlers, Mr. Ross and Trip are wild with joy. Sadie Beagle is most aware that the moment is special. The exuberant gallery is now silently stunned. Like a feather, Uncle Colin picks me up and places me on his shoulders, carries me to Old Dad who joyfully bounces me and throws me to my beaming Dad. When Dad puts me down, Sadie Beagle runs onto the green and makes a huge fuss. As I squat down to pet her, she excitedly licks my face. Looking up to the sky, Hector is circling far overhead and the season's first snowflake hits me in the eye. My Native Americans, colonial settlers and Mr. Ross are gone but I feel them there with me.

A few more snowflakes fall and then it turns into a squall. Jackie says, "Let's get home before this Thanksgiving blizzard hits." With Jackie's permission, Sadie Beagle and I run home through the snowy woods and soon she and I are back at our Crystal Spring WhiteHouse sitting at Old Dad's desk, snuggling on his leather love seat, sipping perfect Jackie hot chocolate, watching the snow cover the seventeenth fairway and preparing for the rest of the sweetest, "funnest" and "bestest" Thanksgiving ever.

Lions and Elephants

Just before dinner, Uncle Colin stops in. He says, "Elizabeth Madeline Black, you have taught me much today and I have shared every concept regarding golf and life that I know with you — save for one. As you know, my college golf teammate, roommate and best friend, Emeric, is from West Africa. Whenever we found ourselves up against it in a match, he would look me in the eyes and say, 'Remember the lion is the king of the jungle but when the elephant walks the earth shakes and the turf forever records his passing.' Then, birdies would begin to fly."

Uncle Colin left and went down for Jackie's Thanksgiving dinner. His message is a bit overwhelming and lost on me. I am chock-full to the brim with birdies, eagles, hawks, beagles, Native Americans, settlers, old Scotts, little boys named Trip and turkey with stuffing. Lions and elephants too — really!

A few weeks later, when I was back in Hawaii, l received a holiday card from Mr. Major James Landing II. On the cover, there was a sketch of a windblown Crystal Spring Golf Club flag caressing a number 8 Callaway. In the background, a hawk can be seen soaring above the late autumn trees. Snowflakes are swirling about. The sketch is signed by Mr. Kevin Hogan, a famous H-town artist, who was in the gallery that day.

On the inside of the cover there was a printed scorecard:

Crystal Spring Golf Club
1982 Thanksgiving Day Tournament

Hole	1	2	3	4	5	6	7	8	9	10		
Par	4	4	5	3	5	3	4/5	4	4	4		
Doc	4	3	5	2	4	3	4/4	4	4	4	37/-3	
Maddie	4	3	5	2	5	2	5/5	4	4	3	37/-4	(winner in a one-hole playoff)

In the card's center, with a holiday decorated Crystal Spring Golf Club clubhouse as a watermark, Major Jim precisely penned the following note:

12/25/1982

Dear Elizabeth Madeline (Maddie) Black (*HCSGCLCC):

        **HSTBAGC

        **TDCT — TYS

        **HWTCWG

        ***MCAHNY

Very truly yours,

Bolt

Mr. Major James Landing II
PGA Head Professional
Crystal Spring Golf Club

* Honorary Crystal Spring Golf Club Lady Club Champion
** Please see your silver coin
*** Merry Christmas and Happy New Year

Epilogue

Old Dad had nailed it. Every word is as I remember it. It is just as we had reminisced, shot by shot, that post-holiday Friday so long ago.

Clearly Old Dad wrote this story to be about me and not about him and that is a bit sad because he, the "almost" Senior Club Champion, is the real "character." Primarily for my amusement, in a fun attempt to put me off my game and to get me seriously accustomed to the "opponent's needle," throughout the match (and our life-long relationship) he chattered old chestnuts in my ear:

- When putting he would say, "Read it, roll it, hole it."
- When a shot proved spectacular, he would ask, "Lucky or good?"
- With a malevolent smile, he would caution me that my caddie (Uncle Colin), "Reads greens like a bat in a dark room deciphering a Russian newspaper."
- When I was in the rough on five, I heard him just audibly say, "She is again lost without a compass" — so true until Sadie Beagle saved the day.
- When his drive would fly an inch, a yard or a mile ahead of mine, he would announce a "Roy Orbison" or a "Linda Ronstadt" and hum *Blue Bayou* leaving me to figure out his message — "I just blew my drive by you."
- There was the "did you hear they are building a new super Wal-Mart with the largest parking lot in Maryland." And when I would ask, "Where?" with delight he would answer, "Between my drive and yours."
- Whenever his caddie would call out his yardage to the pin he would predictably declare, "My favorite number."

- When I was guilty of an errant shot, he would emit an irritating great-grandmotherly, "Oh my my" or counsel, "Some do believe perfect is the enemy of good."
- When my game needed a boost, with a wink he would advise, "Maddie, you should lay off for a week or two and then quit."
- To fool me into thinking he was losing confidence, his would roll out his sketchy Irish brogue and feign lament, "If I could just once play my usual game."
- And, for the unprepared, there was the surely lethal, "Maddie do you inhale or exhale when hitting the ball?" The first time, it took me a week to get over that.

That Thanksgiving Day Uncle Colin had a tonic and antidote for all of it. And prepared well by my dad and my Old Dad, that day, and throughout life, I fell for none of it.

Over the years, I have often been asked about my most memorable moment on the golf course. Expecting recollections of a memorable match, people are a bit surprised when I relate — "I was five and visiting Grandmother Jackie and Old Dad. It was late May and Uncle Colin was home from college. Old Dad was to come home early from the hospital and the four of us were to squeeze in 18 holes before dark. Old Dad and I would be teammates in a two-man scramble (as young children, Old Dad always had us play scrambles, "So we only have to remember our good shots") with the losers cooking dinner and doing the dishes. My kindergarten competitive juices were pumped. But, overnight and all day there had been a steady rain. When the time came to play, Major Jim was forced to officially close the soggy course. I, crushed by disappointment, began to bawl. Old Dad picked me up, wiped away my tears and in his perspicacious way said, 'Maddie dear, I must now teach you the power of doing the opposite.' Soon we had our golf rain gear on. With an excited very young Sadie Beagle leading the way, we headed to our Crystal Spring stream to 'go fishing.'

As if it were today, I remember the warm gentle rain on my face, the sound and vibration of huge drops tapping on the brim of my cap and noggin, the glorious smell of the course in full bloom and the soggy turf beneath my feet. Our usually quiet, steady brook was bounding. Its crystal clear rushing water had exposed golf balls that had been buried in the stream's bottom mud. With 'fishing pole' in hand — an old persimmon driver with top carved out to scoop balls — I set about 'the sacred work of rescuing and rehabilitating lost golf ball souls.' For hours, I became one with nature. Time stood still. In the gloaming, I was warmly soaked to the bone and Sadie Beagle and I became newly close friends with ducklings, fawn, gosling, kits, snakes and muskrat. Like me, each seemed so comfortable and unafraid. Together we rejoiced in the rain's power to enable our 'doing the opposite.' As I slept so well, I dreamt of them that night."

Our family has been powerfully influenced by Old Dad's "do the opposite" message. Several years later, we were delighted when Seinfeld's George Costanza mastered doing the opposite. When we pointed out to Old Dad (a huge Seinfeld devotee) that his philosophy may have been stolen, he led us to believe that he may have shared it with the Seinfeld team; that he and Jerry may be best buddies; and, insinuated within the insinuation that Jerry may rarely make a significant move without first checking with him — just another example of Old Dad masterfully and effectively blurring reality, creativity, imagination, possibility, ability, motivation and attitude — Old Dad's lasting gift to his patients, colleagues, friends and family.

Six years after our Thanksgiving match and the summer before my senior year in high school, I was playing in a regional ladies' championship at a historic, staid and prestigious golf club in the Western Pennsylvania Laurel Mountains. With two holes to go, I was quite unbelievably (even given my infinite optimism) tied with a lady whom gentle Grandmother Jackie would kindly describe as a "rough old girl." She was everything I was not — a mature, majestically leonine seasoned champion who was confident the tournament was hers for the taking — a lioness of golf if you will.

It would be indelicate for me to repeat what she said to me on that 17th tee so I will just say, as an exercise in expert bullying and intimidation unfolded (Ben Hogan's "out play, out work and intimidate them"), I was introduced to a new word or two. And right then and there, Uncle Colin's long forgotten words came back to me and brought me peace, "Remember the lion is the king of the jungle but when the elephant walks the earth shakes and the turf forever records her passing" — and birdies began to fly.

Several hours after the match, the lioness called me at home and apologized for her unsportsmanlike behavior. That phone call started a true friendship that lasts until today. Over the years, when partnered as teammates, we proved there are times when it is good for even a "lady" elephant to have a "rough old girl" lioness at her side.

As you know, I go by E Madeline Black MD and the E is for Elizabeth. At the Naval Academy when my teammates got wind of the Colin/Emeric lion/elephant story (from Old Dad no doubt), they began to say E stood for Ellie as in Elephant Madeline Black. It got to the point where many thought my first name was Ellie. Even now, these many years later, I fondly answer to either Ellie or Maddie.

As I have gone through life, from time to time I have sensed Native Americans and colonial settlers at my side. Often, Sadie Beagle is there too. It happens in the heat of battle when a patient's life or a match is going in the wrong direction. The sense of their presence calms me, enables me to offer my best effort and allows my inner ability, motivation and attitude — my humble greatness — to express itself. I observe we humans have a capacity to carry our ancestors and the distant past within us to assist us with the complexities of our present. At times, I sense our progeny and our future are somehow here in our present too — ah but that is a story for another day.

E Madeline Black MD
November 2012

Acknowledgements

From inception to completion of *A Crystal Spring Thanksgiving,* I am indebted to my senior editor Ms. Maureen Theriault, my golf editor Mr. Colin Michael White, my graphic artists Mr. Kyle Haught and Ms. Susan Shaffer and my webmaster Mr. Lucas Mumford for their immense talent, dedication, applied wisdom and valued good counsel.

Then there is the long gray line of master mentors that have shaped my lifetime learning, teaching and learning. With some semblance of classification and chronological order: White, Collins, Sherman, Martiniano, Walker, Aumiller, Woodriffe, Forsythe and Crivella; Clemens and Hemingway; Scheffer, DeVita, Furth, Goodman, Scharfman, Tartaglia and Bernene, Crosby, Anderson (W), Holzinger, Leach, Simmons, Roth and Wong; Alfonsi, Lasek and Mertz; Anderson (R), Hamill, Heatherington, Howard, Jones, Moyer, Ott, Petrick, Rowe, Wellinger, Welliver and Wright; Bremmer, Carder, Como, Culler, Devers, Dobson, Farkas, Fetrow, Galligan, Gaudy, Ghobrial, Helfrick, Hightower, Hirsch, Khaja, Kellis, Leverett, Lippman, Menon, Miaskiewicz, Navarra, Palmer, Pohland, Rice, Rothrock, Rotz, Sollars, Towe and Zoretich; Duval, Price, Shorto, Zinchini, McConnell and Schouller; Hogan, Rotella, Penick, Owen, Ross, Bell, Rose and Feherty; and, Ahmad, Ahmed, Clair, Drawbaugh, Guidry, James, Kleppick, Leff, Mumford, Obringer, Sandhu, Senan, Sweeney, Uzicanin, Wilson and Zampelli. Any wisdom in *A Crystal Spring Thanksgiving* emanates from their grace on and off the course.

Dr. Mike White

T Michael White MD

Dr. Mike White is a general internist who lives in Hagerstown Maryland. His professional career has addressed private practice, academic medicine, departmental leadership, medical education, hospital administration and healthcare consulting.

He is the author of *Unsafe to Safe — An Impatient Proposal for Safe Patient-centered Care*. A third book (working title *Letters to an Aspiring Physician*) is nearing readiness for publishing. Its goal is to encourage the young person aspiring to a career in medicine to courageously pursue that dream.

Dr. White and his wife Jackie live along Donald Ross' Fountain Head Country Club in Hagerstown Maryland. They are the parents and grandparents of champion golfers. Each season Dr. White strives to be the senior club champion. To date, he has yet to once play his usual game.

Made in the USA
Charleston, SC
18 December 2013